THERE'S

SOMETHING

ABOUT A

LIBERAL

W. H. von Dreele

Illustrations by Mary Gauerke

ARLINGTON HOUSE
New Rochelle, N.Y.

Introductory Note

There really *is* something about a liberal, and Bill von Dreele is by all odds the best qualified man I know to isolate this quixotic quality and put it to verse, just as Mary Gauerke is the best qualified artist I know of to *draw* it out. If you don't believe me, I respectfully refer you to the absorbing pages which follow. They certainly will appeal to all conservatives and even to that rarest of breeds—the liberal with a sense of humor.

BARRY GOLDWATER

Library of Congress Catalog Card Number 74-134850

ISBN   0-87000-111-6

MANUFACTURED IN THE UNITED STATES OF AMERICA

Contents

THE MIGHTY MIDDLE

On breezeways, porches, lawns and stoops
They contemplate the funny groups.
They watch the wild "Chicago Eight";
They follow Father Groppi's fate.
From 9:00 to 5:00 for half a life
They serve the boss and soothe the wife.
They file in April every year;
They try to push the kid's career.
At 65, they hope to be
Allotted some prosperity,
And brother, what a stink they'll make
If they don't get a fairer shake.

MOONSTRUCK

Crescent, harvest, half or full,
Gently exercising pull,
Someone's playing peekaboo:
Mr. Nixon's stuck on you.

WHEN HAROLD WILSON BLEW HIS BLOODY TOP

Well, God, it's *awkward*. Every bloody ship
Is forced to sail around the bloody Cape!
Damn all Egyptians. (If I were to whip
A squadron into reasonable shape . . .)
Was Eden *right*? Ye gods, I've often wondered.
Imagine Suez British! Aden, ours!
Disraeli would have managed it; I blundered.
(This is *not* one of England's finest hours.)
Will everybody kindly *quiet down*?
Apparently de Gaulle will live for*ever*.
He thinks he's Charlemagne! (I'd like to crown
His Majesty the next time he says "never.")
Damn Ian Smith. Damn Franco! (By the way,
Let's get this straight right now: Gibraltar's *mine*.)
Must *everything* be "Made In U. S. A."?
Where is my tea? No! I shall *not* resign.

CASE DISMISSED

There's still a most unpleasant smell.
I grant you, Teddy's been through hell,
But if *I*'d missed that bridge, I think
I'd write these verses from the clink.

THE McNAMARA LEGACY

The Defense Department appears to be too much concerned with the procedural methods rather than the real issue. Today it would be impossible to get the Department of Defense to authorize the Nautilus.

—Adm. Hyman G. Rickover

When McNamara took the con
(With a heave-ho and a ship-ahoy)
He ran a frugal Pentagon
(It's cheaper mopping up with Joy).
When queried who on land or sea
Ran things most cost-effectively,
His intercom responded: Me!
(Sing derry-derry do)

He loved to bellow, Now hear this!
(Some flotsam's floating dead ahead)
At fellows from Annapolis
(Make that a submarine, instead).
He dearly loved the diesel, so
It makes the surface Navy go.
Thank God he didn't like to row . . .
(Sing derry-derry do)

Unfortunately, Russia feels
(Did McNamara walk the plank?)
You might as well use paddle wheels
(I think he's working for a bank).
Instead of diesels, they prefer
To hear atomic engines purr.
Dick Nixon, sir, do you concur?
(Sing derry-derry do)

A BUN IN EVERY OVEN

George McGovern's flipped his lid:
Fifty bucks for every kid!
(Fifty bucks a *month,* that is.)
The conception's strictly his.
Will the new McGovern bill
Put the kibosh on The Pill?
Will the population curve
Take a sudden, upward swerve?
Frankly, folks, it sure beats stocks,
And it's strictly orthodox.

DR. HYDE, MOVE OVER

My fingers tend to tingle;
   My temples often throb.
I'm manic when I mingle;
   I hiss at every mob.
A tendency to mutter
   Cannot be localized.
When Fulbright spouts, I sputter:
   You think I'm polarized?

WE'LL BE WATCHING, MR. FINCH

*You've got de facto segregation in every part of this
country, and we're going to go after it.*
                    —Robert H. Finch

Sounds hopeful, sir. But as you know,
When they withheld Chicago's dough,
The mayor called the President—
Which ended all the argument.
Today, 200 southern schools
(Defying Justice Warren's rules)
Must integrate each native son,
Or no more dough from Washington.
So, sir, to be consistent, you
Must integrate the Yankee, too.
We'll know you really mean it when
You cancel cash for Darien.

I, A HONKY

Yes, I have read the Moynihan Report.
Consider me forewarned on Baldwin's "Fire."
I note the obviously warm rapport
As Stokely and the bearded one conspire.
I'm knowledgeable, too, about Rap Brown;
I've watched the happy hunters in Detroit.
I realize that burning up a town
Is recompense for honkies who exploit.
Each age has tribulations, I suppose:
It wasn't fun for Guelph or Ghibelline.
Nor do I look complacently at those
Whose journey ended at the guillotine.
However, though their violence was vile,
At least they burned the country up in style.

TELL ME WHY

Tell me why the stocks decline;
Tell me why your welfare's mine;
Tell me why the pound is through,
And I will tell you just why I.O.U.

GLAMOUR ISSUES

The Xerox Corporation has withdrawn 3,000 reprints of an 1895 English edition of Mother Goose's Nursery Rhymes and Fairy Tales, *following a complaint that it contained anti-Jewish and anti-Negro material.*
— New York Times

Children everywhere, be *wary*.
Master Sprat and Mistress Mary,
Plus that frightful kid in blue,
Push a most corrupting view.
Never sit upon a tuffit.
Tell Miss Muffit she can stuff it.
(She digs segregated dives
On the roadway to St. Ives.)
Don't chant ". . . meeny, mynee, mo."
It's *sick*—like a Minstrel Show.
Shoot all mice who run up clocks!
(Mice might munch on Xerox stocks.)
Picket farmers in the dell;
They're all bigots, can't you tell?
No one plays it fast and loose
Like that racist, Mother Goose.

PUSEY'S SOLILOQUY

I do not like their faces. Is it hate,
Or is it just the hair? (Good Lord, J. Press
Is doomed.) They say I must negotiate,
But are they, rather, saying: acquiesce?
O, for a harmless panty raid again!
Damn Nixon. Backbone must not be confused
With raw repression. I remember when
A freshman always begged to be excused . . .
They tell me Eric Sevareid's implied
I pulled a Munich. Well, he's sold out too.
The Corporation's restless. Could they hide
A hankering to tell me that I'm . . . through?
Hogwash. But must the students be so *rough*?
My name in Nathan Pusey, not MacDuff.

THE CRUELEST BLOW

*Gov. Ronald Reagan called today for the Federal Gov-
ernment to make President Nixon's birthplace in the
Orange County community of Yorba Linda a national
historic site.* —New York Times

Anoint the Harding house, or pour
    Libations over Hoover's home.
Let's all collectively adore
    Cal Coolidge in his catacomb.
Praise Taft, for heaven's sake, or say
    A prayer at Bill McKinley's shrine.
But don't ask liberals to lay
    A wreath at Nixon's. No. *Non. Nein*!

CRIMINAL JUSTICE

Bobby Kennedy is dead;
Sirhan shot him in the head.
This I know because TV
Made the shooting clear to me.
Sirhan even tells us *why*:
Kennedy was doomed to die
All because he couldn't hide
Cheering the Israeli side.
Will the lawyers, therefore, mix
Sirhan up with politics?
Silly! He's a *paranoid*.
Stamp the kitchen shoot-up "void."

HIGH NOON AT THE *HEW* SALOON

The doors swing in, the doors swing out
And still the cowpokes talk about
The way the Westerner subdued
That busing-crazy Eastern dude.

They didn't actually *draw*.
They sort of sat there, jaw-to-jaw.
One helped himself to something, neat,
Then (POW!), the other hit the street.

Some say he did it with his boot.
The gals insist he didn't shoot.
I know the boys were set to lynch
The dude (that's Allen), but for Finch.

21

A MODEST PROPOSAL

My radio is Japanese.
For all I know, my BVD's
Are products of an export plan
Originating in Japan.

The Datsuns and Toyotas soar
As Ford and Chrysler mop the floor.
Does anybody think we can
Do something, soon, about Japan?

I know progressives get alarmed,
But if the Japanese rearmed,
They'd export less—and Nixon-san
Could crawl back in the frying pan.

AN AMERICAN DILEMMA

Often I have been challenged during these twenty years to come back and to review my findings in the light of all that has happened since I left the scene of my study. I have felt tempted to do so. But I have found it impossible . . . —Dr. Gunnar Myrdal

My Dear Dr. Myrdal:
I know how you feel.
Reviewing a thesis has little appeal.
You wrote it, we read it, and now it's the law.
Why bother with bigots who fear there's a flaw?
There's much to be done and there's so little time,
So onward and upward: you're still in your prime.
South Africa beckons; Rhodesia, too.
The Hindus and Moslems need guidance from you.
Be bold! Be audacious! Be *brutal* with blight.
But get out of Sweden. (It's hoplessly white.)

THE FINAL SOLUTION

De jure's forbidden; de facto's OK.
Stop fussing and feuding! They *want* it that way.
Instead of repeatedly blowing your cork,
Start swinging de facto, like folks in New York.

CONSIDER THE LOBSTER

*Large male lobsters cannot mate with smaller females,
yet they drive the smaller males that can, away. The re-
sult is that the female, who can only mate for a single
48-hour period every two years, loses her big chance.*
—Dr. Saul B. Saila, University of Rhode Island

Girl lobsters are crustaceans which,
When their libidos start to itch
(Bi-annually, kindly note)
Find meaningful romance, remote.
Then too, sophisticated males,
The kind with really *gorgeous* tails,
Can't manage to be indiscreet
With females which are too petite.
Moreover, complicating this,
The bulls express a prejudice
Toward younger males designed for fun
Who, unromantically, run.
I'm sure the female lobsters fret;
(I *know* the males are all upset).
Their nerves must pay a frightful toll . . .
However, they've got birth control.

CRAZY LIKE A FOX

As I smilingly approve
Every crafty Nixon move,
Shall I place him on a par
With that master, FDR?

LET'S HEAR IT FOR MARK CROSS

You know this store? The salesmen *never* brag.
Six years ago, they banned the 'gator bag.
They did it so the alligator could
Be nasty, like an alligator should.
This week, the ladies got another shock:
Mark Cross just put the kibosh on the croc.
Hurrah! I unreservedly concur.
Now let's do something mean to Jackie's fur.

MILTON FRIEDMAN KNOWS BEST

Open the spigot. Loosen the locks.
Something's not working. (Look at my stocks!)
Business is lousy. Borrowing's *hell*.
Brokers are bleating: What's there to sell?
Please, Mr. Nixon, now that you're in,
Don't let a Hoover horror begin.
Listen to Milton; he's in the know.
Make with the moola! Let yourself go!
Give us a dribble . . . even a drop.
Otherwise, kindly pass us the mop.

SELF-DIAGNOSIS

I burp at breakfast; belch at lunch.
I'm off my feed. I've lost my punch.
My ganglia are out of whack.
I'm restless when I hit the sack.
I itch . . . I retch . . . I don't feel well!
I'm up to *here* with Charles Goodell.

NO ESCAPE

The surprising discovery of high insecticide levels in fat tissue of polar bears deserves special attention.
  —Dr. Charles J. Jonkel, Canadian Wildlife Service

The condor's eggs are cracking;
    The bass is belly-up.
There's DDT for tracking
    Within the buttercup.
Crustaceans in the ocean
    Imbibe a bit each day.
There's poison in the potion
    A chicken chews to lay.
The research with tomatoes
    Suggests some residue.
It's present in potatoes.
    Ye gods, it's in me, too.

MIDDLE-BROW ME

I shall not carp about Bob Hope.
    If they adore Red Skelton, *swell.*
I'm not among the snobs who mope
    When Guy Lombardo casts his spell.
If Billy Graham's dining in;
    If Pat digs cops in peacock-blue,
I find the scene more genuine
    Than what I've been accustomed to.

GOD BLESS OUR INSECT FRIENDS

The wasp, it has a fearful sting;
    The yellow jacket's painful, too.
When bugged, the honey bee will cling
    Until she gets a howl from you.
Eschew the gnat; do not abuse
    The horsefly passing on the wing.
Be fair when broadcasting the news:
    The Agnew stings like *anything*.

WILL SOMEONE TELL ME WHOM IN BLAZES THE NATIONAL COUNCIL OF CHURCHES THINKS IT REPRESENTS?

Some things I'm very vague about,
    Like why the Incas fell.
Did Garbo do . . . or didn't she . . .
    With John . . . in *Grand Hotel?*
The Kremlin's an enigma, and
    A Powder Room is, too.
One doesn't gab with oracles;
    A harem is tabu.
What happened to Miss Earhart, the
    Authorities can't say.
(We'll never know what Mrs. Lin-
    Coln thought about the play.)
And as for Council fathers, they're
    The *oddest* mystery.
I don't believe they speak for God:
    They sure don't speak for me.

I'LL GIVE YOU ODDS

If Illinois were told to do
What Mississippi's going through,
I think the absence of applause
Would even make a Percy pause.

POOR BABY

Representative Ogden R. Reid (R., N.Y.) decided to cancel a scheduled trip to South Africa after he learned that the South African government would grant him a visa only on the condition that he made no speeches.
—N. Y. Times

There's so much to ogle at Kruger;
    The fauna are truly bizarre.
While elephants stare,
You're in for a scare
    As lions paw over your car.

The veldt is a vision at sunset;
    The bush is a hunter's delight.
Pretoria's where
The Boers, in their lair,
    Gave Britain a hell of a fight.

It's oodles of fun for the tourist;
    Each province has something to teach.
So come and compare,
By ship or by air . . .
    Unless you're intending to preach.

HUMPHREY SINGS "MY WILD IRISH ROSE"

My wife takes Compoz
When threatened by my prose.
>   Though I research with care,
>   All the tots seem to stare
And the old geezers doze . . .
The crowd holds its nose
When I belt out my prose:
>   Have I made a mistake?
>   Could it be I should take
A broom to my wild, styleless prose?

SPRINGTIME IN NEW YORK

Sooty snowdrops; grimy crocus;
Aching eyeballs out of focus;
Steamy effluence in sewers;
Furtive filthy-picture viewers;
Daddies fuming to be ferried;
Bodies begging to be buried;
Wheezing emphysema cases;
Screaming sirens; frightened faces.
All the while the winds deliver
Greetings, from across the river.

CHRISTMAS IN NEW YORK

Wheezing, sneezing, eyeballs smarting,
Christmas in the city's starting.
What's the mean monoxide rating?
Jing! Jing! Jing! It's *stim*ulating.
See the funny war dissenter
Kick a cop at Lincoln Center;
See how everyone turns waxy . . .
Better call yourself a taxi.
Now it's off to do some shopping;
Now it's homeward, nearly dropping.
With the packages you're lugging,
You're a candidate for mugging.

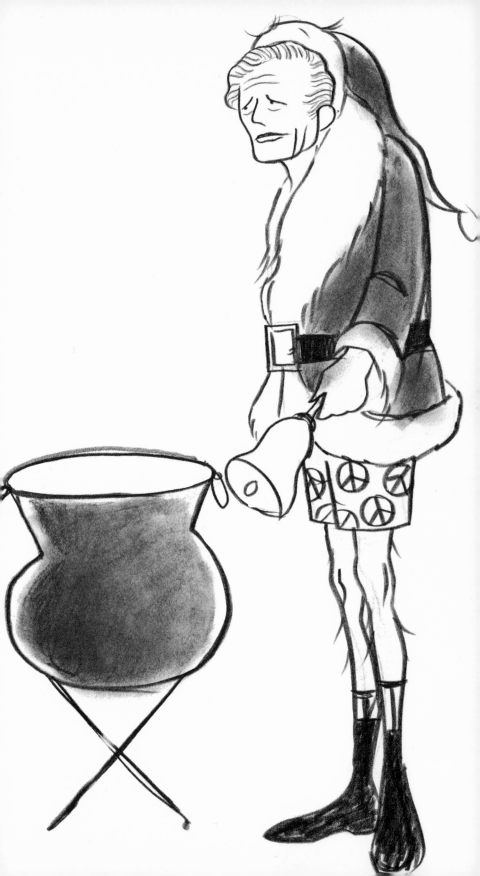

LOOTERS WILL BE SHOT ON SIGHT

(American: archaic)
In 1945, I did some looting.
We called it "liberating" then, of course.
If some civilian talked of prosecuting
We always had the luxury of force.
I own some lovely linen and a rifle.
The latter's lined with silver on the stock.
We looted a Mercedes for a trifle,
Along with half a cellar of Medoc.
What times we had! I savored every hour.
The Hun was on the run, and it was *fun*.
By April, all the Rhineland was in flower
And I was in the army which had won.
Today, the way each youthful looter's treated,
I've learned to sympathize with the defeated.

THESE MEN ARE DANGEROUS

Twelve self-appointed Mr. Cleans,
The *Wednesday Luncheon Group* convenes
Each week in Washington to map
What to endorse and what to scrap.
To name a few, there's Edward Brooke,
Jack Javits, Percy, Cooper, Cook,
Goodell and Hatfield, Clifford Case . . .
All pop-eyed over Peace and Race.
Though only 12, they pack a punch.
For instance, over Wednesday lunch
They hog-tied Haynsworth; Carswell, too.
Therefore, some fall, if I were you
I'd make the rascals face the truth—
Then nail them in the voting booth.

NIXON AT THE TILLER

I try to dampen any doubt
As, getting set to come about,
He runs before the wind instead.
Then, sensing something dead ahead,
He jibs . . . and with the rail awash,
Begins to point to windward! Gosh,
I'd hate to sever my support,
But starboard's right and left's to port.
Will someone tell the captain, please?
The crew's becoming ill at ease.

ON THE PASSING OF PRINCES

"Camelot is on the moon."—Eric Sevareid

I have not been among the masses who
Applauded any Kennedy in view.
When Jackie spoke, instead of going ape,
I usually looked for an escape.
And so, again, as morbid millions stare,
I'd like to comment briefly on the heir.
Unlike Prince Charlie, bested at the Borne,
He doesn't have the luxury of scorn.
No French asylum comforts him off-stage;
Yet, like the Stuart, he's outlived the age.
Now will the mass hysteria subside,
Deflated by a midnight auto ride.
Indifferent, the people fail to swoon:
Their Camelot is moving to the moon.

SUICIDE NOTE IN THE FORM OF A SONNET FOUND ON THE ASPHYXIATED BODY OF A FAMOUS LIBERAL

The beast is in. Four years to go, ye gods!
(I cannot take four years of Dr. Peale.)
What's wrong, America? I give you odds
He'll press the button by September. We'll
Be vaporized, of course, and serve us right.
Poor Hiss . . . poor Helen Douglas . . . *Emigrate*:
(I'd do it, but it gets the wife uptight).
Two bits they tune in Lawrence Welk at 8:00!
Pablo Casals, where are you? Robert Frost?
The Cabinet is *ghastly*. (Middle Class,
I give you Richard Nixon.) We are lost.
Seal up the windows, please. Turn on the gas.
    We're destined to be governed by a jerk
    Elected by the stupid clods who work.

THERE'S SOMETHING ABOUT A LIBERAL

He's bored by columnists who log
The horrors happening in Prague,
But merely touch on Ian Smith
And he's off on the Hitler myth.

When buffeted by campus blacks
He's usually making tracks,
But say you're sorry for the South
And he'll be running at the mouth.

However, to conservatives,
The weirdest wrinkle's where he *lives*.
It isn't where they're all uptight;
It's where the neighborhood is white.

STRAIGHT TALK FROM ABE RIBICOFF

Rejoicing's in order, so let us rejoice.
Abe speaks with an unhypocritical voice.
If mixing's the message, let's mix up the whole;
No chef ever beat up just *half* of a bowl.
I'll turn on the blender; you watch the dough rise.
Perhaps we'll concoct a delightful surprise.
But if the ingredients stick to our plates,
We'll bloody well eat it in all fifty states.

GREY EMINENCE

France's King had Richelieu;
    Wilson had his Colonel House.
Harry Truman took advice
    From his spouse.

Hindenburg had Ludendorff;
    Castro had the *New York Times*.
Louis let La Pompadour
    Ring his chimes.

Ibn Saud caucused with
    All the gals he could afford.
Mitchell's Mr. Nixon's man . . .
    Thank the Lord.

THROUGH CAMBODIA WITH WALTER CRONKITE

A signal sent by semaphore
　　Is sometimes misconstrued;
In Italy, the signaling
　　Is often rather lewd.
That night on the *Titanic*, all
　　The dots and dashes failed.
(Occasionally, using smoke
　　Beats memos that are mailed.)
The radio is prejudiced;
　　One dare not trust the press.
I guess that leaves just pigeons, since
　　I can't *stand* CBS.

TALKING DIRTY

I am no stranger to the dirty book.
I've run through all the early Henry Miller.
When pictures pass my way, I take a look.
I separate the filthy from the filler.
The cinema I've contemplated, too.
I've witnessed Warhol's worst, from drag to stag.
I read *The Village Voice*; I gawk at *Screw*.
I'm titillated by Hugh Heffner's mag.
But recently, lasciviousness palls;
It's difficult unearthing something "better."
I think (it's *crazy*) literature calls . . .
I'm rediscovering *The Scarlet Letter*!
However, while I'm certain lust's a bust,
It's definitely hellish to adjust.

BURIED

George Gallup says the likes of us,
By 8 to 1, don't want to bus.
Where did I read your thoughts and mine?
The *New York Times*, page 49.

WC PROBLEMS

Admittedly, I'm looking wan:
A bomb exploded in my john.
It wasn't in my building, but
Concussion's got me in the gut.
Why must the men's room be the place
To blow us into outer space?
If they're determined to go BOOM,
I wish they'd use the ladies' room.

HOW I SURVIVED THE GARBAGE STRIKE

You've heard about the awful time
    We had in New York City . . .
The mice were big as melons, and
    The rats attacked my kitty.
Park Avenue was perfumed with
    A most peculiar fragrance.
(Some say it should be bottled, since
    It kept away the vagrants.)
Thank goodness I discovered a
    Procedure to control it!
I locked my garbage in my car
    And someone always stole it.

THE LAST ACT

Let the velvet curtain fall;
    Drag the creature off the stage;
Stifle every caterwaul;
    Hoist the integrated cage;
Clang the iron hinges shut;
    Make the combination whirl!
This may be illegal, but
    For my money, so was Earl.

THE BRIGHT SIDE

I do not beam at Nixon's team.
There's been no sign from Herbert Klein.
(Otepka's in, so I should grin?)
And Robert Finch won't give an inch.
However, though I fail to glow,
It's comforting to see the string
Of writers *sick* because of Dick.

AREAS OF AGREEMENT

Senator Cooper and Senator Church
Couldn't care less about who's in the lurch.
Rather like Senator Borah, they think
Foreign entanglements lead to the brink
(Always excepting entanglements we're
Knitting together with Golda Meir).
Nevertheless, for their push to reclaim
Some of the Senate's eroded good name,
Let us applaud! We've been holding the fort
Ever since Franklin tried packing the Court.

CORPSES ON THE MEKONG

While Charlemagne was battling to bar
The Norse from navigating up the Seine,
Cambodia was building on a par
To rival anything Parisiènne.
Still standing north of modern-day Phnom Penh,
More vast than Egypt's Karnak, Angkor Wat
Recalls a race we shall not see again.
Combative as the fabled Hottentot,
They occupied Siam. They chose to squat
Four centuries atop the Vietnamese.
Unfortunately, now they sense a plot
To bracket *them* between parentheses.
And thus, within a sonnet's measured space,
I've told it all—and scarcely mentioned "race."

THE NEW ECONOMICS

Round about the cauldron go;
In, the funny figures throw.
Toe of Amex, nail of Dow;
Sweat from Richard Nixon's brow.
Season with consumer's ear
And a fingerful of fear.
Add a cup of Standard Oil:
Stir, until it starts to boil.
Once the bubbling begins,
Kenneth Galbraith always grins!
That's because he'll recommend
Tax and tax and spend and spend.

THE GREAT PUT-ON

Some fishes simulate a rock
When danger throws them into shock.
Zoologists are known to err
When naming pandas Him or Her.
A bobwhite plays at being sick;
A lizard imitates a stick.
And where's the kid who hasn't read
About a possum playing dead?
In nature, creatures find it wise
To cultivate a good disguise,
But watching Lindsay blow the scene
Beats anything on Halloween.

ALBERT GORE EXPLAINS

I voted for Abe Fortas;
    I'd vote for him again.
I know he stashed a bit of cash,
    But what a legal pen!
I voted NAY on Haynsworth;
    I vetoed Carswell, too.
I'll specify my reason why
    So y'all won't misconstrue:
Their rulings are the *dullest*;
    Their reasoning, I shun . . .
Now don't be snide and say that I'd
    Have black-balled Washington.

ENNUI

Mr. Palme, who's the leader
    Of the see-no-evil Swedes,
Hopes Hanoi is hailed The Winner
    And the NLF succeeds.
As he showers them with krona;
    As his population cheers,
Think how *boring* to be neutral
    For 150 years.

YUMPING YIMINY

Not since Waterloo have Swedes
Soiled themselves with martial deeds.
No one seemed to suffer pains
Watching Bismarck rape the Danes.
Similarly, Sweden passed
When the crazy Kaiser massed.
Nor did Norway's awful fate
Make the Swedish escalate.
Finally, they've struck a blow!
Sweden's recognizing Ho.

POSITIVE THINKING

With Lindsay in and me without
A victory to crow about,
It's tranquilizing to recall
How Spiro drives him up the wall.

DR. GOLDWATER, CALL SURGERY

Although I live in New York State,
I'd cheerfully accept my fate
If Barry sawed the seaboard off
And watched us vanish in a trough.

YARBOROUGH BITES THE DUST

Did somebody pass him the Black Spot?
    Or was it a witch on the range?
Did Someone Above contribute the shove?
    (I've *more* that I'd like to arrange.)
Perhaps there's a Yarborough dolly
    That Nixon's been sticking with pins . . . .
Whatever the cause, it's given a pause
    To others with liberal sins.

BLESS 'EM ALL

Hard hats in Mayor Lindsay's town
Can put it up or tear it down.
Sometimes they sweat; sometimes they freeze.
They do not dangle Ph.D.'s.
They do, in an old-fashioned way,
Appreciate the U.S.A.,
And what a groove it was to watch
The weirdos get it in the crotch.

AMUCK

They marvel at his Spanish;
    His packaging is slick.
Yet invitations vanish . . .
    The entourage is sick.
Caracas sent a veto.
    They banned him in Peru.
The Army's out in Quito.
    Bolivia withdrew.
It isn't halitosis.
    It's surely not BO.
Nor is it a neurosis,
    Since Happy is in tow.
The President is quiet.
    (Reporters tend to cluck.)
Nobody loves a riot.
    The Rock has run amuck.

THE TROUBLE WITH ROCKEFELLER

Four generations since the old man died:
I still remember scenes on Pathé News
When Rockefeller Senior would divide
A dozen dimes among the caddy crews.
His seed is everywhere. One grandson reigns
In Arkansas; another rules at Chase.
In Albany, a third says he disdains
Ambitions for a Presidential race.
O Lord, give Nelson strength in his resolve;
Help Happy carp in harpy fashion, No!
Illuminate the way he likes to solve
Insolvency by squandering more dough.
If they recalled that dollars come from dimes,
I think they'd panic at the *New York Times*.

HINDSIGHT

As trousers wax and minis wane,
The men grow morbid. I'll explain.
Pear-shaped or apple, *derrières*
Promote the pinch; invite the stares.
But girls: the secret which exerts
This fascination is the *skirts*.
Encased in leggings, what was cute
Makes man a monumental mute.
Therefore, a little hindsight, please!
No gal looks good in BVDs.
And rare's the guy who gets the hots
For pants or trousers or culottes.

MARGARET MEAD GOES TO POT

I "grew up" in New Guinea
    With Dr. Margaret Mead.
I must admit I blushed a bit
    About this island breed.
With Margaret in Samoa
    I "came of age" there, too.
(I think I thought the natives ought
    To rate more acts taboo.)
Now Margaret, pushing eighty,
    Is also pushing pot.
She favors grass for kids in class.
    I think she should be shot.

THUMBING HOME

The historical record will probably prove that in the first hundred days President Nixon made the critical decision to end the Vietnam war, one way or another, and face the political and historical consequences.

—James Reston

If your thumb is in the dike,
What would pulling out be like?
If de-thumbing should begin,
Would the sea come rushing in?
How about just halfway out?
Would the water start to spout?
(Mrs. Gandhi has a thumb,
But salt water makes her numb.)
As for simply sitting there,
Dikes give Fulbright *mal de mer.*
Watch for oceans white with foam:
Mr. Nixon's thumbing home.

BIAFRA FALLS

It's over. Let us offer thanks
To British cash and Russian tanks.
The oil, so precious to the health
Of Britain and the Commonwealth,
Is safe again with British Shell.
The Ibos may not fare so well,
But Harold Wilson says he'll chide
All victors bent on genocide.
It's curious: Above the stench,
Untypically, stand the French.

THAT'S SHOW BIZ

I've never doubted Ronald Reagan's powers.
For me, the fellow's message never sours.
I kept my money on him at Miami;
I'd back him done in black-face, singing *Mammy*.
Now Frank Sinatra (lately of the Rat Pack)
Has hung his hair piece on the Reagan hat rack.
If Mother Rose and Sammy Davis follow,
We'll beat the ruddy liberals all hollow.

TEDDY ON TV

I wondered: would he call for faith
    Or simply summon in the wreckers?
I half expected "Edward VIII"
    But wound up contemplating "Checkers."

THOUGHTS ON WATCHING A HARVARD DEAN BEING EXPELLED FROM HIS QUARTERS

It's difficult, while being shoved downstairs,
To manage the appearance of Who Cares?
While, rearward, wildly hairy and uncouth,
Forever yammering about their youth,
Behold, The Kids—*impossible* to placate.
There was no choice: the fellow had to vacate.
And so, his mien suggesting how they bore him,
The Dean's expelled, like lesser deans before him.
Appalling! Still, I'd be the rowdy messenger
If they'd let me foreclose on Arthur Schlesinger.

EVEN-HANDED JUSTICE

Rebecca, cranking up the well
Way back in ancient Israel,
Would fill her buckets happily,
Then tote them even-handedly.
Today, as Mr. Nixon sticks
To even-handed politics,
I make myself a tiny bet
That Jacob Javits gets us wet.

DEATH AND TRANSFIGURATION

It would be a death-knell for the Republican Party [led by Senator Marchi] in this city to fall into the hands of its right-wing elements. —N. Y. Times

Indulge me, will you, while I plug
Some thoughts about a crawling bug . . .
Just as the caterpillar swoons
Voluptuously in cocoons
Anticipating how he'll fly,
Transfigured, as a butterfly;
So I, a poor conservative,
Demoralized by gun and shiv,
Am itching for the bulletin
Proclaiming Mr. Marchi's win.
Fun Cityites, have you been mugged?
Have brazen burglars got you bugged?
Vote Lindsay out so we can sing
The joyous: Death, where is thy sting?

JANUS FROM ARKANSAS

Why does J. William Fulbright press
The Vietnamese to coalesce?
What do the communists possess
    That's so appealing?
A coalition's right for *them*,
But if you push the stratagem
For Golda in Jerusalem,
    He hits the ceiling.

FEDERAL MONEY

Now watch; I'll draw a diagram.
You give one buck to Uncle Sam.
He gives the dollar back, but it's
Deflated now to just six bits.
You wonder where the quarter went?
To keep the bureaus affluent.
So when they pass it back as "free,"
Restrain yourself from squealing, Whee!

TOWARD A UNITARY STATE

Electoral reform? Don't chuckle, chum.
You're knocking "an idea whose time has come."
It passed the House, though seventy demurred;
It's possible the Senate has concurred.
Now watch the pressure build upon each state
Until three-quarters of them (38)
Abolish the electors from the scene.
Then, rid of that archaic in-between,
The people will be grateful for the chance
To vote exactly as they do in France.

OUR YOUNG WRITERS

"Don't trust anyone over thirty and don't trust anyone
who isn't high."

—Anonymous

De Quincey was a junkie from way back,
While Coleridge was partial to the poppy.
To Burroughs, being out on bivouac
Meant lots of laudanum. Poe just got sloppy.
It's obviously possible to find
Important literati who got "high."
Marcus Aurelius will come to mind . . .
(Count Casanova stuck to Spanish Fly.)
My hang-up is, we've done all this *before*.
Let's face it: freaking-out is hardly *new*.
De Quincey "eating" opium's a bore
And (personally) Ginsberg's boring, too.
Call me old-fashioned. I prefer to glow
From Chivas Regal, or, perhaps, Old Crow.

UNDER THE DOUBLE STANDARD

The two Israelis languishing
    In Syrian detention
Have roused the pilots of this world
    To root for intervention.
Their reasoning is logical:
    Unless the laws are tougher,
They'll soon be flying solo, and
    The industry will suffer.
My problem is their languor when
    The languishing was Tshombe's.
Back then, they navigated like
    A bunch of flying zombies.

ALAS, HARASS

Why is it folks of every class,
Instead of harass, say harrass?
In Gotham, where the teachers blast
The mayor when they feel harassed,
I work off my embarrassment
By muttering, it's harassment.
But how can I instruct the masses
If Lindsay, too, intones "harrasses"?
It's harass! Webster's quite clear-cut.
"Harassing" gets me in the butt.

WOOL-GATHERING WITH JOHN LINDSAY

Damn Nelson. Ye gods, I hate that town.
He's getting on . . . does Happy notice? (How
That bastard would have liked to turn me down!)
She *loved* my sideburns. Brother, what a row
I'll have with Rent Control. *Call Alex Rose.*
Can Rocky pull it off again? Perhaps . . .
They say the kids at Hunter liked my clothes.
Goodell's natty dresser . . . No more flaps!
I cannot *bear* another resignation.
Think peace: Try to remember that. Shall I
Go Democrat—this week—on *Face the Nation*?
These shirtings suit me. Mary knows a buy.

DIEU ET MON DROIT

In Britain, they don't mess around.
When Wilson's Labor Party found
The "coloreds" pushing 3 per cent,
Most colored immigration went.
Now Edward Heath, who'd much prefer
To be the Queen's First Minister,
Endorses bounties for each black—
Provided they'll agree to pack.
Meanwhile, for members on each aisle,
It's very much the current style
To posture, carry on and *scream*
At Capetown's all-white cricket team.

FORGETFUL

Today, tomorrow and next week
Look for the liberals to shriek
Unceasingly about the way
The fellows in the Kremlin play.
Next month, some murmurs may persist.
But by October, "coexist"
Will once again be just routine
For Fulbright, Javits and Eugene.

AT THE WAILING WALL

There shall be weeping and gnashing of teeth.
                                          —St. Matthew

     Senator Javits: "It's a disgrace."
     Senator Percy (turning to Case):
     "Ribicoff did it." Proxmire: "*Yes.*"
     Senator Church: "I call it a mess."
     Senator Griffin: "Who would have thought
     Senator Mansfield could have been bought?"
     Senator Pell: "*I'm* willing to bus."
     Tydings: "And leave the driving to us?"
     Senator Scott: "Let's go for a drink.
     Anyway, Dick was with us . . . I think."

A GIFT FROM SANTA CLAUS

For Dr. Spock, a man of childish sins,
My gnomes suggested open safety pins.
But I preferred a gift that's really living;
As RCA would say, "that keeps on giving."
And so I thought of something *diabolic*:
I'm giving Spock a case of constant colic.

OUR NATION'S CAPITAL

The homicides are up a third;
The rapes are up a fourth. You heard
About the Russian attaché?
The doorman stood just *steps* away . . .
A gal's a goose to lug a purse:
The bags get snatched (and vice-verse).
Department stores go dark by nine;
It's risky going out to dine.
Though liberals may make a face,
The nicest people carry Mace!
So, when those cherry buds uncurl,
Stay home; you're safer—thanks to Earl.

AN APPRAISAL

Martha Mitchell, though you raise
    Lots of people's gorges,
You're the Martha I appraise
    On a par with George's.

GONE ARE THE DAYS

They're tinkering with Stephen Foster:
    Everything's improved.
"Old Folks At Home's" been fumigated!
    (Massa talk's removed.)
"Oh, darkies how . . ." and "am a-ringing"
    Will no more offend.
"Dat mournful sound's" upgraded; it's the
    Pluralistic trend.
How nice to know that "Swanee River's"
    Dialect is Go.
But 15 years from now, will kids be
    Singing "Old Black Joe"?

HERE COME DE JUDGE

*Chief Justice Earl Warren has accepted the chairman-
ship of the International Board of Overseers of the In-
ternational Center for the Advance of Peace, now near-
ing completion on Mount Scopus in Jerusalem.*

—N. Y. Times

He wouldn't know an Arab from
A dromedary's hump.
When rifles crack, who guarantees
His ganglia would jump?
His Hebrew's rather sticky and
His Arabic's a flop.
He couldn't tell a mullah from
A Jaffa traffic cop.
But will this worry Warren? No.
He'll shortly set a date
When Arab and Israeli will
Be told to integrate.

THE MOURNERS

In '48, when Masaryk
Descended (with a helping kick),
The liberals were simply *sick*.

In '56, when Russia's will
Left Budapest supremely still,
The liberals got very shrill.

Today, in '68, as Prague
Recedes behind the Russian fog,
The liberals are all agog.

Depend upon it: when Bangkok,
Arabia, Suez, Iraq
Are Russian, they'll go into "shock."

TEE HEE

There's no undoing Gettysburg
    Or losing Mobile Bay.
Atlanta burned and Scarlett learned
    To put her pride away.
It does no good to glorify
    Manassas I and II;
Despite the dash, without the cash
    There was no follow-through.
I don't pretend the President
    Is Beauregard or Lee,
But watching guys who wipe their eyes,
    It's fun to say, Tee-Hee.

THE GLEAM IN HUMPHREY'S EYE

Hubert Humphrey has a plan:
    When this lousy war is over,
Ghettos will be spic 'n' span;
    Appalachia, in clover.
Tell you what he's gonna do:
    Once the countryside relaxes,
Hubert will present to you . . .
    Taxes! Taxes! Taxes! Taxes!

URBAN RENEWAL

In Charleston, Ansonborough was a slum
Decaying on the Cooper, columns sagged
And pediments were clearly out of plumb.
The borough was a quarter mothers tagged
"Unsuitable." The prudent did not stroll.
But what a treasure! Frequented by men
Who gloried in a gilded girandole,
It was an architectural Amen.
Incredibly, the past is ebbing back.
A Manigault, and then a Middleton,
Reoccupied some buildings that were black;
Held on six years; and, gloriously, won.
      Unlike uprooted blacks in New York City,
      The former occupants are sitting pretty.

WHAT A WAY TO GO

Some die (like Crete) sublimely fast
    By natural catastrophe.
Some struggle gamely to the last,
    Like Harold fighting Normandy.
Some compromise themselves away;
    Some slide beneath a weakened will.
How odd to contemplate decay
    While trumpeting one's overkill.

ON DECLARATIONS

Declaring holidays are best!
    I also love to pass the cup
For dividends declared to crest
    When everything is up.

Napoleon enjoyed declar-
    Ing everyone in Europe "free,"
While Keynes declared that laissez-faire
    Is sheer apostasy.

Declaring bankruptcy's a bore;
    Declaring war is mankind's curse.
But I believe what Lord Balfour
    Declared was even worse.

COUNT YOUR BLESSINGS

Let's contemplate the awful fate
Of people stuck in New York State,
Where twenty million aching backs
Bend under Rockefeller's tax . . .
Remember, as he runs rough-shod,
That there but for the grace of God
Go all of us, with shoulders bent,
Had Rocky wound up President.

111

MINNEAPOLIS ELECTS A COP

Minneapolis, a nation
In the wilds of Minnesota,
Put a warrior in office
To be Keeper of the Arrows;
Placed a brave in opposition
To the City Council pow-wows;
Shocked the Farmer-Labor Party;
Stunned Republican officials.
Chieftains liberal in spirit
Wonder whether it's an omen;
Wonder why a placid people
Liked the slogan, "Law and Order."
They consulted Happy Humphrey
And the hoary hunter, Harold;
Took to wearing totem trinkets;
Studied entrails in the wigwams.
Still, the smoke across the mountains
(Many moons across the mountains)
From the tribes by far Pacific
Spells the awful letters, YORTY.

IF SOMEBODY DOESN'T STOP THIS THING, I'LL PULL THE CORD

Hurry up and shoot the stork:
We're eight million in New York
(With a tendency to sprout
In concentric circles, out).
Hippies, hangers-on and bums
Battle in the seething slums,
Ringed by rivers *eels* abjure,
They're so stinkingly impure.
Meanwhile, where the monied meet
On East Sixty-Something Street,
Matrons find it hard to bear
Breathing our polluted air.
That's why I've been seeing stars.
I'm with Agnew. On to Mars!

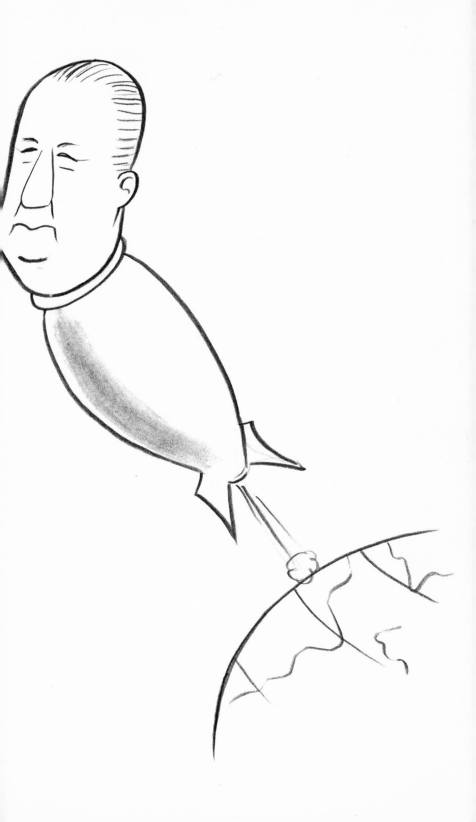

CONSOLATION

When epidermis layers itch
And ganglia begin to twitch,
I mitigate my misery
By thinking of Max Rafferty.

When arches ache and temples throb
As I survey the fickle mob,
I soothe my sensibility
By thinking of Max Rafferty.

If fears about the coming scene
Are shading *your* complexion green,
Remember Thomas Kuchel! (He
Was done in by Max Rafferty.)

THE CHILDREN'S HOUR

A drunk is a drag, but heroin's fun.
The Veep is a pig; McCarthy's The One.
Algeria, yes; South Africa, no.
(With Salazar gone, Angola must go!)
Nigeria's right; Rhodesia's wrong.
Fidel is the guy who's singing their song.
They pillory Paul; they idolize John.
They're dying to dump Taipei and Saigon.
With Kiddieland so incredibly *sick,*
I'm doing my thing for Spiro and Dick.

ASCENT FROM CHAPPAQUIDDICK

Teddy, in a stump oration,
Ridicules "Vietnamization."
Hints at CIA collusion;
Darkly prophesies delusion.
No attempt at being subtle:
Teddy's hungering to scuttle.
Funny, what he wants to smother
Had the blessing of his brother.

117

THREE PROPHECIES

Have you read Lenin lately? Lenin said
The *generals* would do the Germans in.
He prophesied disaster dead ahead
Once military planning ruled Berlin.
For England, Lenin traced a falling curve
Descending from the first Elizabeth:
With little on the island in reserve,
The kingdom would *expand* itself to death.
He also had a chilling word to say
About the way the likes of us would end.
America, he said, would pass away
Because of an obsessive urge to *spend*.
Two out of three so far! That's quite a score
For someone who passed on in '24.

SHOW US A SIGN

Like Elijah, who implored
"Water for my people, Lord,"
I've been dying on the vine
For some Presidential sign.
Just a tiny one would do:
Say a cloud across the blue
(Scudding left to right, of course);
Something *solid* to endorse.
What a joy, therefore, to say
Nixon's making rain today.
For a Presidential "sign,"
Mr. Justice Haynsworth's fine.

LET'S NOT KID OURSELVES

Who feels a thrill recalling when
      D'Estaing appeared off Sandy Hook?
Who cares what Rochambeau did then?
      Who marvels at the risks they took?
Does anyone remember yet
      The signal service of de Grasse?
Or how the touchy Lafayette
      Worked wonders on the Gallic brass?
If lapses such as this assault
      The memory of Uncle Sam,
Will Asiatic hordes exalt
      Our sacrifices in Vietnam?

TOM WICKER ISN'T WELL

The patient's pulse is rapid.
      The respiration's weak.
The eyes are rolling madly;
      He cannot always speak.
The wonder drugs aren't working.
      (The doctor is a *dunce*.)
One remedy will save him:
      Let's integrate, at once.

121

REPRESSION, ANYONE?

Take me back to boola-boola;
    Row me to the Raritan.
Strum a uke for dear old Duke;
    Raccoon it, on rattan.
Tired watching campus cuties
    Brawling for their next degree.
Sock 'em up and lock 'em up,
    Then throw away the key.

RHODESIA, RAMPANT

Polo and cricket and old-school cravats;
Gardens and parties and ladies and hats . . .
Salisbury seems to be having a ball:
Everyone's turning the Queen to the wall.
Gasoline's flowing from devious routes;
Tea from Ceylon is developing shoots.
Furious liberals at the UN
Counted to ten, and they're counting again.
Why do they have such a passion to flog
People in Salisbury rather than Prague?

MAILER FOR MAYOR?

Norman Mailer, whom I've read
Since *The Naked and the Dead,*
Has a platform with some pull—
Interlarded with the bull.
Bureaucrats are not his bag;
Central planning makes him gag.
Norman's slogans really swing:
"To each neighborhood, its thing."
Groovy! Watch the people run
To the segregated one.

124

THINK TANK

(Dedicated to Spiro Agnew)

If Russians genuinely shrink
From confrontation with the Chink,
    I think
The Chink, although a deeper pink,
Could prove a most rewarding link
    To sink
The Russians, shrinking from the brink. . .
Let's not be beastly to the Chink,
    I think?

INVICTUS

I shall not mount the wailing wall
    To fulminate on fouls,
Nor shall I grasp the awful sword
    And plunge it in my bowels.
I shall not throw myself before
    A local on the Pennsy;
I do not go for gesturing;
    I'm strongly anti-frenzy.
No, I shall simply carry on,
    Continuing to screw
The Humphreys and the Muskies in
    The NATIONAL REVIEW.

PREACHER PROBLEMS

Millennia ago, it seems
My minister developed themes
Related to the infinite
As registered in Holy Writ.
He loved to meditate on goals.
He often mentioned saving souls.
Way back then, no one thought it odd
If, once or twice, he mentioned God.
I know such sentiments are square.
I realize it isn't fair
To people under 25
Who simply do not dig that jive.
That's why, for fogies who believe,
At sermon time, it's best to leave.

THEY

They label jellied gasoline
Uncouth; uncivilized; obscene.
They violently disagree
When bombers maul the DMZ.
Haiphong is sacred; so's Hanoi.
When fighters fly near China, boy!
The caterwauling conjures up
A pekinese about to pup.
However, when South Vietnamese,
Eviscerated neck to knees,
Appear (as "filler" in the news)
They never, ever, sing the blues.

BATTEN DOWN

Ease her off and shorten sail;
Obviously, it's a gale.
Who's that hiding in the gig?
Throw the bugger in the brig.
Rig the lifelines; stow the gear.
Shout each order loud and clear.
Oilskins out and hip boots on!
Mr. Nixon has the con.